The Stars of Far Away
A Poetry Collection
By
Maisie Kitton

First Edition.

Pictures/Canva

ISBN: 9798761310940 (paperback)

Available in ebook

Published by Maisie Kitton (on KDP)
@MKitton2206 (Instagram)

For everyone who has yet to find their place,
I believe in you x

Table of Contents

Loveless World

Water rushes over my feet in a loveless world
Where humans and animals suffocate
Amidst the fog that rises from
The bubbling ground.

There's far too much distance between people
While they walk,
Covered in breathing apparatus,
Attempting to protect themselves.

The grass isn't green,
The trees are dying,
And the flowers no longer bloom.
The water's turning brown,
The sky's turning dark,
And the sun no longer rises.

The Burdened Bridge

I'm a wedge between two worlds,
My hands both tied.
Blood mixes inside me,
A viscous fluid at war with itself.
I see two realities at once,
Light and Dark,
And I'm in a perpetual state of transfer.
Not quite here,
Not quite there,
Where am I?

Those who once knew me know not,
Those who once saw me see not.
Nothing more than a ghostly shadow
I drift,
Back and forth and back and forth.
I sit at my desk but it's not me there.
I lay in my bed but it's not me who lays there.
I'm not here,
However, I am,
Drifting and floating and connecting two worlds
That shouldn't be connected.

I shouldn't be here...
But I'm unable to leave,
Painfully wedged in a door that won't close.

Self-Inflicted

Holding my pen so tight my fingers might break,
The bruises stay and hurt and ache
Like any other pain,
Although this pain is different;
It's self-inflicted and I didn't know I was doing it
Until it was too late.
I'm labelled.
I'm tragic.
Don't look at me like that.
It wasn't my fault.
No one was there then,
No one is here now;
What do you expect me to do?
Just stop what's become second nature?
Just stop what's become habit?
I feel sorry for you,
For thinking that I can change just like that.
I feel sorry for you because you clearly don't know
What it's like to be an accident;
What it's like to watch the clock hand tick
another minute;
What it's like to come back to an empty home;
What it's like to feel…
Even if I don't feel anything right now.

A Girl on Fire

The glaring light hits.
My head is set alight a thousand times over.
It roars like thunder and lightning in one,
Its eyes burn with an electrifying craving,
Lips twisted callously,
Desirable and silky,
Tongue darting from the moist cavern like a
threatened snake,
On fire.
A girl on fire.
But when the light flickers and dies the fire
burns out,
Mewls like an abandoned kitten,
Eyes crying for shelter,
For somewhere dry and warm and safe,
Tongue desperately wetting those Neglected lips,
Split and bloody,
Drowning.
A girl snuffed by a flood,
Snuffed because that's what happens to fires,
The sparks of the smallest revolution.
They sputter out,
Spit embers,
And they die.

Divine Hell

Divine Hell.
A wondrous place of suffering and wisdom.
Ash and flesh and blood.
Banished as an innocent child
I was raised by demons and every kind of
Demonic entity.
I was raised by rivers of bubbling blood,
Walls of fire as far as the eye can see.
I was raised on pain,
Fed with despair,
And I slept in an everlasting nightmare.

Unresponsive

I can't get my body to respond.
I need to get up,
Do normal human things,
But I'm not responding to myself.
I'm screaming;
My mouth stays deliriously shut.
My mind shouts;
I drift away.
My entire body feels like lead,
Thick and unmoving and... heavy.
Even my eyelids – just opening them hurts.
When did such a simple task become so daunting?
All I can do is lie here and blink.
I fall asleep.
I wake up.
Still no response.

We Shouldn't Be

When we're drunk I wish I remembered
Why we shouldn't be.

The wisps of restraint roar into
An inferno of interest as soon as
The drink hits the back of my throat.
We're touching each other,
Lost in the feeling of ecstasy.
I want to restrain myself,
To leave,
To never come back,
But the drink shreds my rationality.
It allows me pleasure when it shouldn't.

We're drunk and I wish I
Remembered why we shouldn't be.

You Think I Don't Feel

You think I don't feel anything.
You're sorely mistaken.
I feel too much,
But I can control it,
Let my guard down when I'm alone,
Then.
And only
Then.
When I know no one is watching
I'll let loose a
Scream
That shatters everything in
Its wake.

You think I don't feel anything…
I feel too much.

Release

My muscles ache and clench and
Twist under my skin,
Shaking and trembling with an
Overdose of oxygen.
Or is that a withdrawal?
The universe is in me and I am in it.
My body succumbs to the pulse of
A release and begs for more.
I go back and forth with the feeling
Until I give in completely,
Body limp, slack, open.
It's a sluggish feeling,
Not at all the escape my body craves.

Him

His long fingers play the strings
Like He's a part of the instrument Himself,
Small strokes,
Gentle brushes,
Soft thrums.
Without trying He creates a melody that
burns my soul
And sets my whole world alight.
Each note fuels the fire and
I'm shattering like broken glass,
Crumbling at His feet.
This power He has over me is devastating.
Devastating but addictive.

Orpheus and Eurydice

Play the lute,
Damaged Orpheus,
Let the music flow into the ground;
The world can hear your melody.
It reaches those down with Hades
And feeds them hope.

Damaged Orpheus,
Your weakness isn't like Achilles.
Your music covers it,
Presents it,
And breaks Death's hold of
Beloved Eurydice.

What I See

Trembling fingertips rise to meet
A smooth surface,
Gentle and soft and beautiful.
Orbs that hold oceans and deserts and fires,
All of which spill out into the reality it provides.
No words,
No sound,
No movement,
Just silence, and a little smile,
A little blush, rosy cheeks, bright eyes.
I see an angel on Earth, fire on fire,
Softness and tenderness of desire,
A wilting shadow that blooms and blossoms
Out from the depths of darkness.
I see a flicker of electricity, a spark, in a blackout,
A pinnacle of hope that
There is still something left,
Something left of me.
Your being ignites the smouldering ashes that were
withering,
Explodes them to flames and splintering roars
That spread rapidly in my veins.
Fire flows within me, just as it flows through you.
I see two shadows dancing.
I see shadows morphing with the smoke and the
ripple of flames.
I see you, in your purest form,
Fiery veins,
Blackened fingertips…

… And now so are mine.

I Found You

We met in darkness.

Not a harsh kind,
A soft, slow gloom that churns
Around and around.
It was there.
I saw it.
A pair of gentle eyes that
Shone like scorching flames.
They burned with interest
And I gravitated toward you.

Smooth skin and an easy smile
Greeted me,
A light in the dark,
A burning pyre,
And whenever it gets unbearable
My mind reverts back to that
Moment in time when we
Collided.
Mystery. Intrigue. Fascination.

We collided in the dark,
Planets locked in orbit,
And the dark is where I found you.

Colour Me

Colour Me.
All those blank spots.
All those spaces that lay bare.
My white skin that shines too bright.

Colour Me in.
I want to see how you see Me in both
Day and night.
When it's light and dark.
I want to know if your views of Me change.

Colour Me in full.
I want to see what colours you
Gravitate towards,
What colours you pick out of the
Box before the others.
I can see what colours you are
While you decorate my skin with
Feelings.

Colour Me in,
Just so I feel like I have some feeling.
The colours you choose will stay on Me forever,
Tangible,
Volatile,
Knowing.
They'll complete Me in ways that even I
Don't understand.

Colour Me,
And give Me life.

A Spell

Your eyes cast a spell on me
And I find I can't break the chain.
It keeps me prisoner,
A slave to your love,
But I don't wanna break free.

Your touch encases me in concrete.
I can't move,
Can't scream,
Can't shout.
Poison ivy winds around my body and
My heart starts to pound in my chest.

You force me out of myself when I
Want nothing more than to hide away,
But I don't wanna stop this.
I'm the bear and you're the trap.
Once I'm in there's no getting out.
But what happens if you trapped me
Long before I realised what was happening?
You've trapped me here,
But I don't wanna stop this.
I don't wanna break free.
I don't wanna,
Don't wanna,
Break free.

Anchor

You're my anchor.
But instead of steadying me
You drag me down until
I can't breathe.

Your soft fingers leave bruises where
They crush my ankles too tight.
I can't pry them off
When I'm fighting so hard to
Stay above the water.

Each time my lips breach the surface
I gasp in air.
You yank me down hard,
And salty water inflates my lungs
Before I have a chance to prepare.

My body bucks and lashes out
But you're invisible.
You're an invisible attacker
And the salt hurts my eyes.
I can't see to save my life,
Which is a shame…

Ghost

I fall asleep alone,
Wake up alone,
But there's evidence of your presence;
Minimal washing up by the sink,
Dirty clothes on the bathroom floor;
Wardrobe half open;
Your keys are missing and you've unplugged
Your phone charger;
The bed's cold and I know you must've
Left hours ago,
Before the dark even had a chance to properly settle,
Before the sun even had a chance to breathe.

I never physically see you anymore,
But I see breadcrumbs of your motions.
You leave me this trail to follow.
So, I do,
In hopes that one day I'll find you at the end.
It never happens.
The second I reach the end,
It's the start of another,
And the trail never ends.
You're nothing but a ghost to me now,
A ghost in the land of the living.

Ships

Set in your ways,
Too proud,
Too blinded by your abandon
Of keeping your ship tight.
You sailed with authority
And forgot the majority
Are not like you.

Forsaken Love

We're broken like those picture frames
On the side of the road.
Glass punched in,
Shattered over the floor,
Picture deformed and torn and
Not at all like it was before.
The little birds swoop down
For the glistening shards,
Swallow them whole,
And their deaths are on us.
We turned co-dependency into
A boxing ring except
It's the ropes that hit us,
Beat us down,
Until we're coughing blood onto
A bed of daisies,
Painting them,
Bathing them,
In the essence of
Our forsaken love.

Endless Road to the Sea

The Endless Road to the sea,
It's where you'll find me,
Watching the water ebb
Away, away, away.

We used to walk this road Together,
Now it's a Lonely memory.
Pictures flash before my eyes,
Ghosts of smiles on my lips.

Remember when we used to walk
Down the Endless Road to the sea?
Remember how it was there
That we could truly be?

The truth in me grew
And the devil in you flew,
Away from me,
And the Endless Road to the sea.

Let You Go

Tonight I'm going to let you go,
Set fire to the dying roses on the table,
Drink from the ancient wine glass and
Fill my stomach with the absence of you.

Tonight I'm going to forget you,
Hide away your things in the darkest shadows
I can find and leave them there to rot in the
stifling heat,
Nothing left of them but the charred embers of a once
Roaring flame.

Tonight I'm going to start again,
Light my own fire for my own purposes,
Guide the lost souls back home,
Demand justice for those who fall.

Because tonight I'm going to let you go
And I won't have to see your wretched
Face ever again in this lifetime.
I tip the contents of the glass down the drain
And allow myself to ooze away with it,
Finally free of your prison.

Black Instead of Blue

My blood runs black and lifeless,
As is my life now you're gone.
So free and pure we once were,
So lively and loving,
But it had to end – it was inevitable.
Infatuation and love are two different things,
In fact, the polar opposite;
Something I learned the hard way.

Resent followed and stretched its devilish wings,
Spread far above us, bordered us,
Us against the world.
We breathed the same air,
Content in this safe haven,
Sheltered from our feelings.
Inside those wings we could forget.

Only… those wings sliced down and severed our
hearts in two.
They severed our hearts into dust and thinned my
blood to gloop,
Stringy gloop that holds my body together.
They blackened my blood like smoke and
tar and ash.

Before I could speak those wings came
crashing down,
And now my veins are black instead of blue.

White Flag

I sailed the white flag,
Hoped you'd understand my intentions.
It blinded your view of the dark,
Left me running in its shadow.

A moment in Time

The pictures on the wall depict moments in Time,
Frozen memories that eventually begin to fade,
But the pictures come to life whenever eyes are
laid on them,
Happiness. Contentment. Love. Laughter. Light.
Pinned, stuck, hung on the walls,
Framed up to enhance its value.
A moment in Time.

Two networks possessing one frame,
Two halves of one whole.
A sun diving in the background,
Its light bleeding across the icy floor.
A moon swoops up to its grave on invisible wings,
Silhouettes and Shadows and Shades.

Misshapen shapes that are out of focus,
Sharp features which draw the eye,
Either button or brush it is unsure;
Chance or destiny.
The colours mesh into one distortion flawlessly.

Yet despite the aesthetics, looming doom is taken,
Right from the boundaries and all the way to
the heart,
Fingertips sneaking in from all perspectives,
Dragging. Tearing. Slashing. Defacing.

Once flipped it stops, an overbearing white
staring outward,
Replacing the fingers,
And before long it flips itself back again.

Or it's forced back again, the urge to look becoming
devastating,
The colours and thoughts rushing around, and
around, and –

A moment in Time.

Engravings

By the hill there's a valley, of sorts,
Sheltered by tree roots and leaves and bushes.
The odd spot of light is let in when the wind blows,
Too fast and too rough.
Scratched into the sides of the valley
Are names and dates and faces
Of people young and old.
Fingers trace the lines carved in
Dirt and stone,
Pretending to be the hand of the predecessor.

Headstone

They're natural but not really.
Although they're made from nature,
Evolved and produced from the natural cycle,
These stones are not.
They're manipulated by humans and their tools,
Engraved by human symbols.
They're taken away from nature,
Disrupting the natural cycle,
And are used to measure the length of life and
melting muscles.
They mark the burial site of loved ones,
And the neglected ones,
The ones that no one knows.
They hold meaning beyond comprehension,
Alive and changing since before the birth of
Detention and Rules and Regulations.
They're something solid,
Can easily break,
And smash,
And crash all around
You.

Infection

My clothes shield my skin
From the atmosphere,
From the toxic air we've created.

My clothes shelter my skin
From the acidic rain that falls,
From the evil eye of outer space.

My clothes protect my skin,
But not all of it.
Sometimes it gets through and
Infects me too.

Frost

Crisp underfoot,
Crunches like hazelnuts.
Slips and skids like a caramel slide.
Drizzled atop like desiccated coconut,
Iced like a cake.
Glittering on the floor like sprinkles,
Sparkling under fluorescent lights.
Bitter and cold like iced lemon juice,
Let the frost hang in its noose.

Slip Inside

The bird swoops down and
Slits my throat with
Its beak.
Slashes me, cuts me, defiles me.
Its talons claw my skin and
Pull it apart
Slice by slice before it
Slips inside.
The eyes replace my own and
In the mirror I see the bird in
My own body,
Writhing under my skin.
And there's nothing I can do to stop it.

Ivy

Moss sticks to our feet and
Ivy binds us to the ground,
Digging into our wrists and
Draining our bodies of blood.
It spills into the Earth,
And the soil is damp at our feet,
Those vines of ivy pumping and sucking like
a vampire.
Our wrists ache and a sharp,
Throbbing pain ignites as the vines
Slither deeper into our wrists.
We can see them wiggling under our skin,
Worms and snakes and maggots.
Something that's not me is inside me,
Inside us,
And I can't get it out.
Not without hurting you.

Floodgate

The dulcet melodies settle and calm
My frazzled nerves,
A shell-shocked soldier.
They soften and manipulate my body into
A palpable mess of dead limbs and
Dead weight.
The energy is zapped from me and
I want to sleep.
I want to shut my eyes and drift into
Neverland,
To a world that's leagues away from Here.
I want to lie Here forever and let
Lyrics and notes and music wash over me,
Through me,
Kill me softly,
Not like one of those shells they throw.
String by string,
Word by word,
My body dies and I'm blocked by a
Floodgate.
I'm perpetually trapped Here in this nightmare
And I can't unlock these chains that
Tie me down.
I'm stuck by a floodgate,
Tied to the bottom,
And I fear I might be drowning.

Punishment

I draw the curtains in a broken home
And ignore the angry shouts from Below.
I'm left breathless and gasping for air at the dust
That flies about me, double over, breathe.
The small cries of what once was a bundle of
Joy fills me with dread.
I run to her and pick her up,
Cry silently and beg them to stay Below.
My arms cradle her,
A sobbing mess,
Coated in black and blue,
And I whisper.
Please be quiet. Please be quiet.
She doesn't give.
I rock her,
Hum under my breath,
A tune from a distant memory,
My eyes firmly shut in prayer.
Please. Please.
Silence.
She's staring right at me,
Big blue eyes staring at me in wonder.
Her smile is toothless,
A giggle on her lips.
She stares at me like I'm an angel,
But I'm not.
I'm an angel fallen from grace,
And this is my punishment.

Death Walking

Freshly polished buttons.
Newly ironed jacket.
Rolled up sleeves adorned with golden cuffs.
Silk gloves that swathe spindly fingers.
Plaid trousers.
Shiny black boots.

He walks like thunder,
Smells like lightening,
Has a tongue like Satan.

He carries a knife and
Slaughters those in his way,
Innocent or not.
He's invisible,
Although people say that he flickers into existence
As the victims draw their last breath.

But if you follow the trail of bodies,
The bloody footsteps,
The droplets of blood that drip from his silk gloves,
You might just end up at the
Tip of the blade
Begging for death.

Blossom

Like flaky snow the blossom comes cascading down,
Fluttering and rippling like butterflies.
It lays on a bed of grass if it's lucky;
Most days it floats and travels,
Never finding its final resting place.
Chased by crows,
Hounded by wolves,
It can never settle while in such a fragile state
of mind.

Winter

Arms stuck out of the mass;
Some hanging limply,
Some at right angles,
Some drooping,
Some rigid,
Some carrying heavy burdens.
Some have already lost them to the bitter wind
of winter,
Their corpses rolling and spinning with
Frozen shards chipping off at every
Harsh scrape.

The burdens still there hung so that arms
Dipped lower… lower… and lower to the icy carpet,
Which shot up with white veins gripping
Everything it could touch,
Everything it could control.

Nerve endings tangled themselves into the feet,
Keeping the huge mass rooted to the spot,
Controlling its movements,
Stunting its growth.

Hair hung loosely.
The roots shook.
Were battered. Bruised.
All into unclasping from the dainty fingers;
Wrinkled and holey but strong.

Howls shook the shrivelled strands into stupor,
Each more violent than the last,
Succeeding in ripping them from their
vulnerable stance.

Ripe

The apples are ripe on the tree
But there's no one around to
Pick them.
They've been ripe too long,
Too healthy.
Starting from the core the infection spreads,
Shoots out like arrows,
Striking itself and everything around it.
The juicy redness turns into
A brown mess,
Spitting acid and spilling essence;
We've neglected nature's cycle.
Now we must pay the price.

A Hopeless Spring

The flowers all burn in the snow;
Frozen petals alight;
Stems darkened by black venom;
Its amputated roots struggle to breathe.

The lamb;
A frosty carcass on a bed of ash;
Sticky poison on its lips, tar;
Carved from stone like Pompeii.

The lake on fire;
Dazzled and blinded by the moon;
A dry rain falls from space;
All hail the Mighty Lord.

There's no birdsong here,
It's birdshriek;
Like sirens they scream.
When they sing the tune falters and dies
And blocks their throats until they suffocate.

There's no spring here.
It's a rather hopeless hope if I must say;
There's nothing here but death and fire,
And I think we've finally ravaged her.

Singing

When I come to, I hear quiet voices
Singing fragile songs.
Or maybe I hear fragile voices
Singing quiet songs.
I can never tell the difference.

There's pain,
Oh boy there's a lot of pain.
It lathers my body,
Makes me squirm,
And when the water hits me it's
Scalding hot, scalding hot, scalding hot.
I remember writhing in agony,
A scream,
And empathetic darkness.

The same voices are singing the next time.
The pain is still present in my every limb,
Weighing me down,
Tying me to whatever I'm lying on.
It's not hard and lumpy,
But I can tell you it isn't soft either;
It's not the fluffy blanket my grandmother knitted
For me when I was five.
The thought bores me back to the darkness.

I'm tired the next time.
Bored. Tired. Bored.
It goes in a cycle.
An endless cycle.

I feel the weight of
Bandages on my head,
Covering my eyes,
The emptiness there,
And I wonder what happened.
When I have the strength I touch those bandages
Gingerly with my hands,
The movement stiff and unsteady.
It tires me out and I'm gone again,
Back into the blissful darkness.

The bandages are gone and I think that
I was out for a while.
I blink but it hurts.
I blink but it's a sharp pain.
I blink and nothing changes.

I lie there in darkness,
Not asleep,
Awake.
The awake feels like I shouldn't be and
I want nothing more than for someone to
Peel my eyelids back and let light into my
Black reality.
I'm told that nothing will bring the light back.
I live in darkness now,
And I think I want to hear the people around me
sing,
So I listen,
And I listen.

The men are still singing.
I listen some more.
I want to hear their lyrics now.

Fully grown men babble words,
Mumble, mutter, whimper, cry,
Whisper to the ceiling and to the invisible people
That aren't really there.
Men pray and plead to someone
That doesn't exist.

I sink further into my sheets,
Hope that the darkness takes me away again
Like it's been doing.
The darkness evades me and I have to live
This pain that only I can hear around me.

Days

Day by day
The air gets colder,
Gets slightly choppier,
Like an ocean,
Although they say that the ocean itself
Is getting warmer.
Global Warming, they say.
They also say that we've damaged
Earth beyond repair.

Why did we let it get to this stage?

The cool breeze rustles the leaves and the grass,
Brushes right up and over me,
But not before making sure
I'm blessed with the coolness of its touch.
Its touch cools me down somewhat,
Forces the heat and the sweat away from me.

The sun highlights the different shades of green
On the grass,
The trees,
The trees that should outlive us sevenfold,
And shines down upon clump after clump of
Wild flowers.
No direction,
No restriction.
Just wild.

The wild is still here in this park,
But it's tainted by humanity:

Enclosed by fences and gates;
Built-in goalposts and benches and tables;
Mowed grass...
Although the wild is still alive,
It's being contained,
Controlled,
Directed.

Sparrows and blue tits twitter and hop on the grass,
In large or small groups.
There's safety in numbers after all.

Despite being day the moon hangs onto
The last flickers of darkness.
Chemtrails litter the once clear blue sky,
Reminding everyone that we,
Humans,
People,
Are the dominant force.

And who knows?
Maybe earthquakes and tornadoes and volcanic
eruptions
Are nature's way of saying
'I will always be more powerful'.
There's no way of stopping a natural disaster...

... but we can stop ourselves.

Our Earth

Stand back,
You can see the destruction we,
Humans, have imposed upon the Earth.
Terror.
Heartbreak.
Destruction.
Death.
Shackles.

We've made this world our own,
But only after completely eradicating the world that
Was here
Before us:

Those animals we kicked out of their homes to
make ours;
Those insects we massacred;
Those plants we made extinct;
Those beautiful sounds of nature we swapped out for
Drills and screams and shouts;
The rivers and lakes we blocked off to create
electricity;
The electricity that is slowly crippling the Earth to
its full;
The electricity that completely
Sucks the life out of
Every living thing on this Earth.

Music now is not like the music of nature.
Rap.
Pop.

R and B.
Hip Hop.
Latino…
… Bird song,
Babbling brooks,
The swift whistle of trees as wind flows about them;
All of that is gone, but not completely.
It still lingers, but only in the four corners of
the Earth.
It still lingers in the places that humanity
cannot touch.

The Earth still spins on its disjointed axis,
Despite the skyscrapers and buildings sticking up in
every direction,
Filling the open plains of grass with
Manufactured and tampered stone.
Somehow the Earth still spins just as fast,
Despite everything we made to slow it down.

She will rise again,
Make things the way they were.
Natural. Free. Open.
Not abnormal, captive, closed.

Earth will become natural once again,
Because our Earth isn't what she envisioned;
After all, it isn't our Earth… it's hers.

Smoke

I see it.
Wisps of smoke,
The swirling tendrils of blackened air,
The remnants of a not so distant past...

The foundations of a future not yet
Come to pass.

Grave

I stare at your grave in the dark and think about
All the things I've done for you to end up in there.
It wasn't bad things,
The things I did,
But they most definitely weren't good things either.
They were mediocre,
And everyone knows that mediocre just isn't
Good enough.

I didn't notice your pain,
Your anguish,
Your hurt.
I didn't notice the change in you,
The tiredness in you,
Your exhaustion.
I missed it all.
Like I miss everything,
And now I have to pay the price.

I lay the bundle of fresh roses on the mound where
you lay.
I didn't deserve someone like you, I mumble into the
cold wind.
The stars above glare at me,
Like I'm to blame.
I am.
I didn't notice,
Even if you hid it well.

You deserve the world – but all you got was this.
I gesture to myself;
A bit on the sloppier side,
Not that either of us cared;
Unkempt hair,
Rough beard,
Pasty skin… sallow and sunken.
Especially after the news spread.

I hope you get what you deserve up there.
I rest my hand on the stone,
Feel a jolt run along my skin.
I dip my head, flinching when it happens again.
Stop. Stop trying to talk to me.
It happens again, and the jolt shocks me right to
my heart.

A cloud allows the moon to slink out into the open
air and it beams down on me.
It beams down on me hovering over you,
Your soul and your being,
And it shines even brighter.
Don't do this, I say. *Please just go up already.*

Wind tangles in my hair,
Rain pelts me hard on the face,
Pelts me all over.
Rain forces me to gasp for breath.
My hand never slips from the stone,
And everything stops when it finally does.

The moon hides,
The stars continue to glare,
The endless shocks stop,
The rain recedes into the shadows…
… I'm alone.
And you're still very much dead.

The Green Children

Out on the green they play with pride,
Fast or slow they seemingly glide,
Like birds, flightless or no, they caw,
All the while following playground law,
Of every second of daylight of every single day,
Outside until exhaustion, and then they hit the hay,
One by one they drop off and sleep,
If only the exhaustion didn't run as deep.

Crippled and weary the children grew,
Never again to experience the morning dew,
Locked and hidden and cold and lonely,
All the while wishing to leave, oh if only!
Aches work their way throughout them one by one,
Until only one remains: voiceless, and finally done,
Jealous of the ghosts that play on the green,
It closed its eyes, having already foreseen,
That long ago they would all be reunited,
Themselves merging and twisting in a single flood,
Free of the disfigurement and the cold,
Concealing themselves in the tree of old,
A burst of light and it all reversed,
Joy. Laughter. Love. Happiness. They all traversed.

Now Delight takes its last breath, a pleasure,
All of them finally ready for their next adventure.

Captain

Your Captain calls too early
And hands his hat over to you.
He needs your help aboard the ship,
To help console the confused passengers
That are crossing.
He took you away but it's okay.
You're needed there.
So wear your hat,
Put on your sailor clothes,
And steer the ship away from danger,
My love.
Steer the ship away from danger and
Guide the lost souls home.
It's what you were born to do.

Nomadic Vagabond

Unconquered I take those steps
Closer to my demise.
There's crossfire in my mind,
A war thundering deep inside my skull.
All I focus on is the destination;
Somewhere bucolic to hide my Nomadic soul.
It won't stay put I know,
Stuck in a maelstrom of adventure,
Though I hide it anyway beneath
A steep shelf of crumbling rocks.
It bolts out like a shooting star,
Faster than any manmade mechanism,
And away it goes at the speed of light,
Zipping back and forth,
Spitting dust.
I breathe in the salty air,
Breathe in the wind.
To my next destination I go,
My hands bound at my hips.

Pandora

When we think of love,
There is nothing more purely undreamed of.
We crave the beautiful yet we are shorn of gloves
in winter.
We were crushed,
Our wants never ceasing,
Our treasure, unwoken.
We are museums and drums,
Our hearts beating like our predecessors,
Detained for all eternity.
Pitiful Pandora cries in despair;
We love, despite being broken beyond repair.

Not All Men

The pavement's rough and coarse against
your cheek,
And you leave behind an imprint of blood and dust
and dirt.
Evidence,
If anyone wanted it,
But the rain will wash it away before anyone
begins to look.

Your words are something you've always relied on,
And in that ruthless moment,
They failed you.
He took your silence as consent,
Courtesy of bad education,
And he taught you that silence means yes,
That silence is an answer.

You think back to the moment when it all changed,
When you became another statistic that no one
listened to;

He follows you home,
And when you report it,
They laugh and say you imagined it.
This same guy pinches your breast so hard it
breaks skin
And leaves a bruise.
Evidence.
You're told to not be so dramatic;
Others have it worse than you do.

And then the unthinkable.
You come home bleeding through your trousers.
Your parents tell you to clean yourself up.
That you'll talk in the morning;
The talk never happens,
Forgotten like a fleeting dream;
Burning inside like a firework,
Ready to explode.

Boys will be boys,
Men will be men;
This just happens to girls.

It's not your fault,
But you should have run away.
It's not your fault,
But why didn't you say anything?
Why didn't you report it?
It's not your fault,
But why were you wearing something like that?
Are you sure you didn't give him the wrong
impression when
You smiled at him from across the street?
Where's your proof?

You hear the stories of other girls around you,
So strikingly similar to
Yours;

Clean yourself up,
Dry your tears,
You have to look your rapist in the eye.
It's only fair.
Don't report him,

Because are you sure?
He's so nice.
This accusation could ruin his life!
He grins at you like he did the day before,
The predatory glint alight in his eyes,
His smile,
The lamentable laughter you heard when he bent
you over last night.

Stop being so dramatic.
It wasn't that bad.
People have lost their homes to wildfires and lost
Family members to Cancer and you're still going on
about this?
You went to his house.
You went into his bedroom.
You didn't try to run.
You didn't tell him no.
You let him touch you with those dirty fingers.
You let him do whatever it is you say he did.

Some guy eyes you up at the bar
Too much too often;
You want to leave.
Why are you so suspicious?
Why are you so scared?
Whatever.
Don't walk home alone.
It's stereotypical to carry protection,
So *don't do it,*
But why didn't you defend yourself?

... And you think you may not be completely alone,
Though there's never a confrontation,
And you most likely won't start it.
What's the point?
They think you're lying anyway,
Because not all men.

But way too many women.

Heaven to Hell

She's holding a child.
One not born from consent but
From brute force.
He violated her body
And created a life she didn't want.
She has to live with this,
A child born from the selfish greed
Of a stranger in the dark.
It looks up at her with those
Wondrous eyes,
Trusting and full of love,
And she has to look away.
She can't bear to stare into those same
Eyes that ruined her.
She's ashamed to hate it,
But that thing grew from
A seed she never wanted sown.
That thing,
Living and breathing,
Will always be a constant reminder
Of the night her Heaven turned into
Her Hell.

Ghost of Me

I believe in ghosts.
Not the haunting types,
Although I believe that
Something from the past lingers in the present;
Ghosts of people.

Much like a reflection,
The ghost of me stays silent,
Keeps its head down,
Doesn't initiate contact.
Follows and obeys and endures.

Like darkness,
The ghost of me is not seen.
I am the darkness,
And the darkness is me.

Like a candle I burn,
Slowly but surely,
Convinced of my existence of one purpose.
Burn, burn, burn.

The ghost of me can't be burnt;
Only me in the present can,
But it's my ghosts that carry the scars.
Eschewed, the ghost of me breaks.

The ghost of me follows wherever I go,
A reminder more than a haunting…
… a reminder of the mountains I've climbed.

All I Am

All my life I wanted to be,
And I think maybe I am,
All I am and all I'll be.

You Will Find Me

'I love you more than I've ever found a way to say.'
And with those figures of the past,
The water is cold beneath my raft.
The air I breathe is empty,
Like there's nothing left for the trees, let alone me.
I need to be hidden,
I need to recharge,
Solitude and silence restarts my heart.
I don't expect you to understand,
You with all the plans,
But this is me,
Expressing myself, free.
I am here, just away,
Already drifting from the quay.
So, look into my heart,
And you will find me turning the page on this part.

A Message

Sometimes, choosing love can be daunting. People leave, and you wonder what the point of love is. You think that you won't ever love again because of how much it hurt to say goodbye to that one specific person.

You will heal, and you will find peace.

And if you take nothing else from these poems, please know there is always a place for you in this world. Please know that you're allowed to change your mind at the last minute. Please know that you're allowed to say no. Please know that you're allowed to put yourself first. Your feelings are valid.

You are more important than you might realise.

Choose peace. Choose Kindness. Choose Love. Because loving someone has never been the wrong thing to do.

Ps. Love yourself, and be yourself, because the world needs you.

Xxx Maisie xxX

Printed in Great Britain
by Amazon